W9-BKC-812

brunch

RYLAND
PETERS
& SMALL

LONDON NEW YORK

Louise Pickford

photography by Ian Wallace

brunch

Senior Designer Steve Painter
Commissioning Editor Elsa Petersen-Schepelern
Editor Sally Somers
Production Gavin Bradshaw
Art Director Gabriella Le Grazie
Publishing Director Alison Starling

Food Stylist Louise Pickford
Stylist Antonia Gaunt

The author's moral rights have been asserted. All rights reserved. No part of this publication may be reproduced, stored in a retrieval system, or transmitted in any form or by any means, electronic, mechanical, photocopying or otherwise, without the prior permission of the publisher.

Author's acknowledgments

Many thanks to everyone at Ryland Peters & Small for their support, and of course to Ian, who not only makes the food look fantastic but is always on hand to taste my recipes and give good, critical (and no-bias) advice.

Notes

All spoon measurements are level unless otherwise noted.

Ovens should be preheated to the specified temperature. Recipes in this book were tested with a convection oven. If using a regular oven, increase the cooking times according to the manufacturer's instructions.

First published in the United States in 2001 by Ryland Peters & Small, Inc.
519 Broadway, 5th Floor
New York, NY 10012
www.rylandpeters.com

10 9 8 7 6 5 4 3

Text © Louise Pickford 2001
Design and photographs © Ryland Peters & Small 2001

Printed and bound in China

Library of Congress
Cataloging-in-Publication Data

Pickford, Louise.
Brunch / Louise Pickford ; photography by Ian Wallace.
    p. cm.
    Includes index.
    ISBN 1-84172-212-X
    1. Brunches. I. Title.

TX733 .P58 2001
641.5′3--dc21

2001031858

contents

better than breakfast...

Like most people I know, I often find that breakfast these days is no more than a quick cup of coffee before dashing out to work. By mid-morning my taste buds are wide awake and I'm starving. This is the time of day I have to settle for a quick snack just to get me through to lunch. But on weekends it's a different story. At last there is time to enjoy a late start, followed by preparing something simple and delicious to eat. Brunch provides the ideal stopgap until dinner, but it's more than that. It is a great opportunity to indulge in all those foods we seem to crave the most. All our favorites—bacon sandwiches, waffles with maple syrup, or eggs Benedict—make ideal brunch dishes. I only wish I had the time for such luxuries every day!

Preparing brunch for friends, a partner, or family need not mean a hectic start to the day. Do what I do, which is to relax in bed with a great coffee and then to wander in the kitchen, getting things ready gradually and with minimal fuss. The best thing to do is to choose dishes that can be either made in minutes or prepared the day before and cooked at the last moment. The recipes in this book enable you to do exactly that. I've divided all the recipes into sensible headings, so finding just what you fancy is simple and practical.

Most recipes serve 4–6, as unless you are planning a romantic breakfast in bed, you are more likely to be preparing brunch for a small group of friends. The ingredients can be halved or doubled as necessary. For any meal at any time of the day using fresh, quality ingredients is so important. I know we are all busy, but taking a little extra time to source good ingredients will produce even better results.

Most importantly of all, brunch is a fun meal. Get organized the night before so that on the day you can relax with your guests and really enjoy this little luxury.

soft-cooked eggs

with asparagus

Even as an adult I never tire of dunking toast into the perfect soft-cooked egg. Well, it's even better when you dip in asparagus spears. Remember that eggs need to be at room temperature before they are plunged into boiling water.

Tie the asparagus into bunches of 6 with kitchen twine. Steam or boil for 3–4 minutes until just tender. Drain and keep them warm.

Meanwhile, cook the eggs in gently boiling water for 4 minutes, then transfer them to egg cups. Remove the tops of the eggs with a spoon and add salt and pepper to taste. Serve with toast and asparagus.

24 thick asparagus spears
8 large eggs
salt and freshly ground
black pepper
toast, to serve

serves 4

breakfast

This is so yummy—a gooey, sweet, fruity oatmeal made with your favorite granola mix, soaked overnight in cinnamon-infused milk. Add whatever berries or stone fruits take your fancy.

cinnamon-soaked granola
with fresh fruits

1¾ cups milk

½ teaspoon ground cinnamon

2 tablespoons honey

4 cups good quality granola, or homemade (see method)

1½ cups fresh fruit and berries

extra milk, to serve

serves 4

Put the milk, cinnamon, and honey in a saucepan. Heat until almost boiling, then remove from the heat.

Put the granola into bowls, pour over the hot milk, and let cool.

Refrigerate overnight and serve at room temperature, topped with fresh fruit and berries and extra milk.

To make your own plain granola: Put 2 cups rolled oats in a bowl. Add ½ cup oat bran, ½ cup raisins, ⅔ cup mixed dried fruits, chopped, such as apricots, figs, dates, banana, and mango, 1 cup mixed toasted and chopped nuts, such as hazelnuts, almonds, macadamias, and cashews, with 2 tablespoons each of sunflower, pumpkin, and sesame seeds. Mix well and transfer to an airtight container.

To make toasted granola: Put the oats into a skillet over medium heat and cook, stirring, until toasted and golden. Working in separate batches, repeat with the oat bran, nuts, and seeds. Let cool and store in an airtight container.

omelet
fines herbes

As omelets are best eaten as soon as they come out of the pan, I tend to serve this for no more than two people. For larger numbers, simply multiply these ingredients accordingly.

6 eggs

2 tablespoons freshly chopped mixed herbs, such as chervil, chives, marjoram, parsley, and tarragon

2 tablespoons butter

salt and freshly ground black pepper

a few extra chives, to serve

serves 2

Put the eggs in a bowl, add half the herbs, and salt and pepper to taste. Beat until runny and well mixed. Melt half the butter in an omelet pan until it stops frothing, then swirl in half the egg mixture.

Sprinkle with half the remaining herbs. Lightly fork through the mixture a couple of times so that it cooks evenly across the base.

As soon as it is set on the bottom, but is still a little runny in the middle, transfer to a warmed plate, folding the omelet in half as you go. Sprinkle with chives, salt, and pepper. Serve immediately and repeat with the remaining ingredients to make a second omelet.

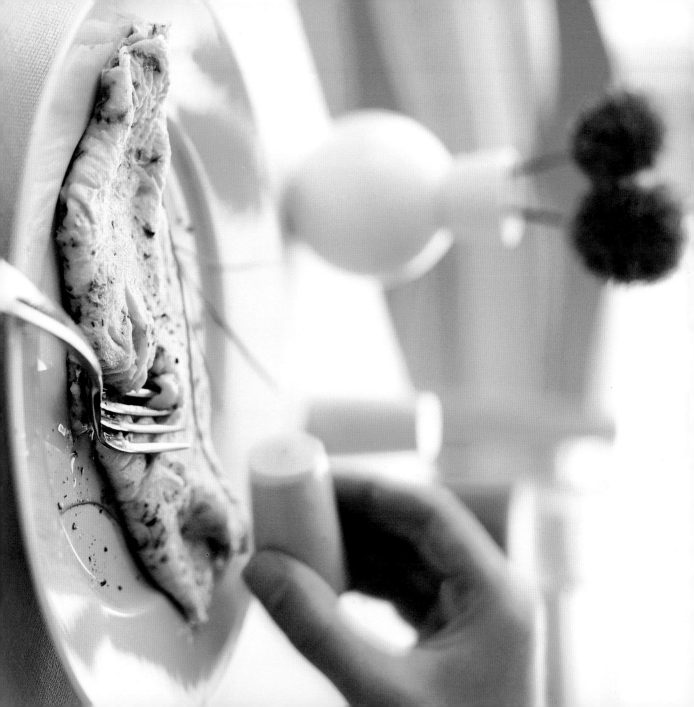

There isn't much to beat figs straight from the tree, bursting with sweetness and a sublime flavor. Look for basket-formed ricotta at good cheese counters.

fresh figs
with ricotta and honeycomb

1 lb. fresh ripe figs, about 8
1 lb. basket-formed ricotta cheese, sliced
a piece of honeycomb or ¼–½ cup honey

serves 4

Arrange the figs and ricotta on a large plate and serve the honeycomb or honey in a separate bowl for everyone to help themselves.

panettone
french toast

with coconut milk

Using coconut milk instead of regular milk adds an exotic twist to this simple breakfast dish.

For a slightly healthier version, serve with yogurt instead of cream.

½ vanilla bean

⅔ cup canned coconut milk

2 eggs, lightly beaten

2 tablespoons sugar

¼ teaspoon ground cardamom (optional)

4 tablespoons butter

8 slices panettone or other sweet bread

to serve

confectioners' sugar, for dusting

blueberries

whipped cream

serves 4

Split the vanilla bean in half lengthwise and scrape out the seeds. Put the coconut milk, eggs, sugar, vanilla seeds, and cardamom, if using, in a bowl and beat well. Pour the mixture into a shallow dish.

Heat half the butter in a large skillet. Dip 2 slices of panettone into the egg mixture and sauté until golden on both sides. Repeat with the remaining slices and serve dusted with confectioners' sugar and topped with the blueberries and cream.

waffles
with maple syrup ice cream

If you don't want to make your own ice cream, use your favorite good quality vanilla, with maple syrup poured over.

ice cream

2 cups heavy cream

1 cup milk

seeds from 1 vanilla bean

5 egg yolks

½ cup maple syrup

waffles

1 cup all-purpose flour

1 teaspoon baking powder

½ teaspoon baking soda

1 tablespoon sugar

½ cup buttermilk

1 egg, lightly beaten

6 tablespoons butter, melted

maple syrup, to serve

waffle iron, lightly greased

serves 6

To make the ice cream, put the cream, milk, and vanilla seeds into a saucepan and heat until the mixture reaches boiling point. Remove from the heat and set aside.

Meanwhile, beat the egg yolks and syrup together, then stir in the heated cream mixture and return to the pan. Heat gently, stirring, until the mixture thickens enough to coat the back of a wooden spoon. Do not boil or the mixture will curdle. Remove from the heat and let cool. Freeze in an ice cream maker, following the manufacturers' instructions. If you don't have an ice cream maker, pour the mixture into flat freezer trays and put them in the freezer. Let the mixture partially freeze, beat to break up the ice crystals, and return the trays to the freezer. Repeat several times—the more you do it, the smoother the end result.

To make the waffles, sift the flour, baking powder, and baking soda into a bowl. Stir in the sugar. Beat the remaining ingredients together in a second bowl, then beat into the dry ingredients until smooth.

Spoon a layer of the batter into a heated waffle iron and spread flat. Cook for about 1 minute until crisp and golden. Serve hot with a scoop of ice cream and a little extra maple syrup.

Note: If you don't have a waffle iron, simply drop a ladle of batter onto a lightly greased, heated skillet and sauté until golden on both sides.

blackberry buttermilk pancakes **with apple butter**

Apples and blackberries are great together, and here a buttery apple sauce tops blackberry-dotted pancakes. Use blueberries or raspberries as an alternative.

apple butter

1 lb. tart apples

3 tablespoons brown sugar

a pinch of ground cinnamon

1 teaspoon fresh lemon juice

2 tablespoons butter

pancakes

¾ cup self-rising flour

1 teaspoon baking soda

3 tablespoons fine cornmeal

3 tablespoons sugar

1 egg, beaten

1½ cups buttermilk, at room temperature

1 tablespoon butter, melted

1 cup small blackberries

oil, for greasing

to serve

light cream

extra blackberries

serves 6

Peel, core, and dice the apples and put in a saucepan with the sugar, cinnamon, lemon juice, and 1 tablespoon water. Bring to a boil, cover, and simmer over a low heat for 15–20 minutes until softened. Mash with a fork, add the butter, and heat through, uncovered, until thickened. Set aside to cool.

To make the pancakes, sift the flour and baking soda into a bowl and stir in the cornmeal and sugar. Put the egg, buttermilk, and melted butter into a second bowl and beat until mixed. Stir the mixture into the dry ingredients to form a smooth, thick batter. Fold in the blackberries.

Heat a nonstick skillet over medium heat until hot, brush lightly with oil and pour in a little of the batter to form a small pancake. Cook for 2 minutes until bubbles appear over the surface. Flip and cook for a further 1 minute until cooked through. Keep the cooked pancakes warm in a low oven while cooking the rest.

Serve the pancakes topped with apple butter, a little cream, and blackberries.

bagels

with smoked salmon and wasabi sour cream

A classic brunch dish given a modern twist with Japanese wasabi paste (horseradish) and sour cream in place of cream cheese.

4 plain bagels

¾ cup sour cream or crème fraîche

2–3 teaspoons wasabi paste

freshly ground black pepper

8 oz. smoked salmon

to serve

chopped chives (optional)

lemon wedges (optional)

serves 4

Cut the bagels in half and toast lightly on both sides. Put the sour cream or crème fraîche and wasabi paste in a bowl and beat until evenly mixed. Add freshly ground black pepper to taste.

Spread 4 bagel halves with the wasabi mixture. Top with the smoked salmon and chives, if using, then add the remaining bagel halves. Serve with lemon wedges, if using.

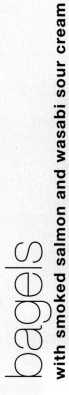

classic brunch

eggs benedict

I usually sauté the prosciutto so it becomes really crisp, adding a lovely texture to the creamy sauce and egg yolks. Try substituting smoked salmon for the ham or, for a vegetarian version, replace the ham with wilted spinach.

4 large slices of prosciutto

4 eggs

4 English muffins

hollandaise sauce

1 cup (2 sticks) unsalted butter

3 egg yolks

2 tablespoons water

1 teaspoon freshly squeezed lemon juice

salt and cracked black pepper

serves 4

To make the hollandaise sauce, put the butter in a small saucepan and melt it gently over a very low heat, without letting it brown. Put the egg yolks, water, and lemon juice into a blender and process until frothy. With the blade turning, gradually pour in the melted butter in a steady stream until the sauce is thickened and glossy. Transfer the sauce to a bowl set over a saucepan of hot water. Cover and keep the sauce warm.

Broil or sauté the slices of prosciutto until really crisp and keep them warm in a low oven. To poach the eggs, bring a saucepan of lightly salted water to a boil. Add 1 tablespoon vinegar, preferably distilled, and reduce to a gentle simmer. Swirl the water well with a fork and crack 2 eggs into the water. Cook for 3 minutes, remove with a slotted spoon and repeat with the remaining 2 eggs.

Meanwhile, toast the muffins whole and top each with a slice of crisp prosciutto. Put the poached eggs on top of the ham. Spoon over the hollandaise, sprinkle with salt and pepper, and serve at once.

Note: to poach eggs in advance, follow the directions above and as soon as the eggs are cooked, plunge them into ice water. Just before serving, return them to a saucepan of gently boiling water for a few seconds to heat through.

mushrooms
on toast
with melted cheese

Large, juicy mushrooms need little embellishment—just a slice of cheese and a hint of sweetness from the brioche.

8 portobello mushrooms, wiped and trimmed

½ cup butter

4 slices of brioche or whole-wheat bread

4 oz. Taleggio cheese

salt and freshly ground black pepper

serves 4

Melt the butter in a skillet, add the mushrooms, and cook for 8–10 minutes, until golden and beginning to give up their juices. Add salt and pepper to taste.

Meanwhile, toast the brioche slices on both sides under a broiler. Spoon over the mushrooms and their juices and top with the Taleggio. Return the topped brioche to the broiler for a few seconds, so that the cheese just begins to melt. Serve at once.

homemade baked beans

1 small ham hock, soaked overnight in cold water

3 cups canned borlotti or Great Northern beans, drained and rinsed

1 garlic clove, crushed

1 onion, finely chopped

2 cups vegetable stock

1¼ cups strained tomatoes or tomato purée

2 tablespoons molasses or black treacle

2 tablespoons tomato paste

1 tablespoon dark brown sugar

1 tablespoon Dijon mustard

1 tablespoon red wine vinegar

freshly ground black pepper

toast, to serve

serves 6

Drain the soaked ham hock, wash, and pat dry. Put into a large, flameproof casserole dish.

Add the drained beans and all the remaining ingredients to the casserole dish. Cover and bring slowly to a boil on top of the stove, then transfer to an oven preheated to 325°F, and bake for 1½ hours. Remove the lid and cook for a further 30–45 minutes, until the sauce is syrupy.

Remove the ham hock to a board and cut any meat into slices. Put the toast onto serving plates, top with the beans and slices of ham, and serve hot.

Soaking the ham hock overnight removes excess salt from the meat. Traditionally, dried beans would have been used for Boston baked beans, but using canned reduces the cooking time by two-thirds.

hash browns

with sausages and oven-roasted tomatoes

A good breakfast for when you're feeling a little the worse for wear—great comfort food.

1½ lb. baking potatoes, such as russets, peeled and diced

4 tablespoons butter

1 large onion, finely chopped

12 good quality breakfast sausages

2 tablespoons olive oil

2 cups cherry tomatoes

1 tablespoon balsamic vinegar

salt and freshly ground black pepper

serves 4

Cook the potatoes in a large saucepan of lightly salted boiling water for 10–12 minutes, until almost cooked through. Drain well and mash coarsely.

Melt the butter in a large nonstick skillet and gently sauté the onion for 15 minutes, until soft and golden. Add the potatoes and some salt and pepper. Cook, stirring and mashing the potatoes occasionally, for 15–20 minutes, until well-browned and crisp around the edges.

Meanwhile, put the sausages in a roasting pan, drizzle with half the oil, and roast on the middle shelf of an oven preheated to 400°F for 25 minutes.

Once the sausages are in the oven, put the tomatoes in a shallow oven dish. Drizzle with the remaining oil and put on the top shelf of the oven after the sausages have been cooking for 5 minutes. Cook for 15 minutes, drizzle with the balsamic vinegar, and let cook for a final 5 minutes.

Spoon the hash browns onto plates, and top with the sausages, tomatoes, and their juices.

kedgeree
with tea-smoked salmon

Tea-smoked salmon replaces the more traditional smoked haddock in this version of the classic English breakfast dish.

3 tablespoons butter

1 onion, finely chopped

1¼ cups basmati rice

1 tablespoon curry paste

4 cardamom pods, crushed

1 cinnamon stick, crushed

1 teaspoon ground turmeric

2¼ cups fish or vegetable stock

tea-smoked salmon

1 lb. salmon fillet

½ cup rice

½ cup tea leaves

½ cup brown sugar

salt and freshly ground black pepper

to serve

2 hard-cooked eggs, peeled and quartered

1 tablespoon chopped fresh chives

1 tablespoon chopped fresh parsley

serves 6

Melt the butter in a saucepan, add the onion, and sauté gently for 5 minutes. Add the rice, curry paste, and spices, stir once, then add the stock. Bring to a boil, cover, and simmer over a very low heat for 20 minutes.

Meanwhile, to smoke the salmon, cut the fillet into 4 equal pieces and sprinkle with salt and pepper. Line a wok or a large Dutch oven with a sheet of aluminum foil and put the rice, tea leaves, and sugar in the bottom. Arrange a rack over the top. Cover and heat for 5–8 minutes, until the mixture starts smoking. Slide the fish fillets, skin side down, onto the rack, cover, and smoke over a high heat for 4 minutes. Remove the wok from the heat but leave undisturbed for a further 3 minutes. Remove the fish and keep it warm.

Skin and flake the salmon into large pieces and add the pieces to the spiced rice. Add salt and pepper and mix briefly with a fork. Cover and leave for 5 minutes. Serve topped with the egg quarters and sprinkled with chopped herbs.

Caesar salad is a classic brunch dish and here the original is jazzed up with fresh crabmeat. You will need good quality crabmeat, so look out for fresh (not pasteurized) lump crabmeat at your fish store.

crab caesar

To make croutons, cut the bread into cubes. Put enough oil in a skillet to cover the base, then heat until hot. Add the bread cubes and sauté, stirring constantly, until evenly golden and crisp. Drain on paper towels.

Put the egg yolks, mustard, lemon juice, and cayenne pepper in a bowl and whisk until blended. Gradually whisk in the oil in a steady stream, until the sauce is the consistency of a thin mayonnaise. Add salt and pepper to taste. Remove a third of the sauce and reserve for another dish. (Cover it with plastic wrap and refrigerate for up to 3 days.)

Tear the lettuce into bite-sized pieces and put in a large bowl. Add the croutons and half the crabmeat. Add the rest of the crabmeat to the remaining two-thirds of the sauce and mix well.

Pour the crabmeat sauce over the salad and toss gently to mix. Top with the anchovy fillets and serve.

4 thick slices of white bread, crusts removed

2 egg yolks

2 teaspoons Dijon mustard

2 tablespoons freshly squeezed lemon juice

a pinch of cayenne pepper

¾ cup extra virgin olive oil

3 romaine lettuce hearts

12 oz. fresh crabmeat

12 anchovy fillets in oil, drained

salt and freshly ground black pepper

vegetable oil, for frying

serves 4

early lunch

BLT tortilla panini

Large flour tortillas make perfect wraps—these are filled and then cooked on a stove-top grill pan for a yummy toasted sandwich.

Put the bacon in a dry skillet over medium heat and cook gently until golden and crisp.

Put the tortillas on a work surface and arrange 4 bacon slices down the center of each one. Top with the tomatoes, cheese, lettuce, and mayonnaise, lightly sprinkling with salt and pepper as you go.

Fold the edges over to form a wrap and cook seam side down in a hot stove-top grill pan for 2 minutes. Flip and cook for a further 2 minutes on the second side. Serve hot.

16 slices bacon

4 large flour tortillas

4 ripe tomatoes, sliced

4 oz. Gruyère cheese, sliced

2 cups crisp lettuce, shredded

¼ cup mayonnaise

sea salt and freshly ground black pepper

serves 4

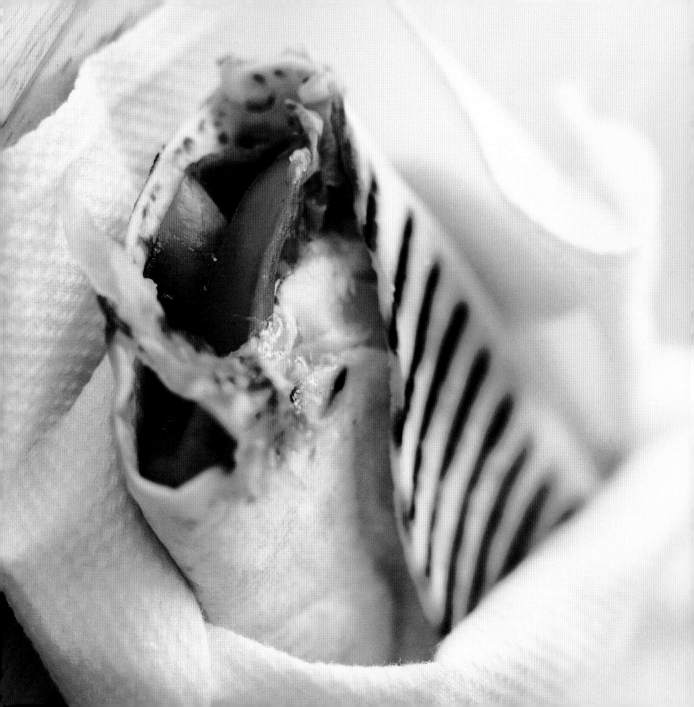

mushroom burgers
with caramelized shallots and garlic mayonnaise

You can keep leftover mayonnaise covered and refrigerated for up to three days.

4 portobello mushrooms, trimmed

1 tablespoon extra virgin olive oil

4 large ciabatta rolls

salt and freshly ground black pepper

mixed salad, to serve

caramelized shallots

1 tablespoon extra virgin olive oil

4 oz. shallots, thinly sliced

2 tablespoons red currant jelly

1 tablespoon red wine vinegar

garlic mayonnaise

1 egg yolk

1 garlic clove, crushed

1 teaspoon freshly squeezed lemon juice

a pinch of salt

⅔ cup light olive oil

serves 4

Heat the oil in a small skillet, add the shallots, and cook for 15 minutes. Add the red currant jelly, vinegar, and 1 tablespoon water. Cook for a further 10–15 minutes, until reduced and thickened. Add salt and pepper to taste and let cool.

To make the mayonnaise, put the egg yolk, garlic, lemon juice, and salt in a bowl and whisk until blended together. Gradually whisk in the oil, a little at a time, until thickened and glossy.

Brush the mushrooms all over with the oil and sprinkle with salt and pepper. Add to a nonstick skillet and cook for 4–5 minutes each side. Cut the ciabatta rolls in half and toast on a preheated stove-top grill pan. Put the mushrooms on 4 of the toasted ciabatta halves and top with the caramelized shallots, mayonnaise, and the remaining ciabatta halves. Serve with a mixed salad.

The eggs are cooked quickly in very hot oil, giving them an almost lacy look and lovely crisp texture.

frazzled eggs

with smoked bacon

2 tablespoons whole-grain mustard

1 tablespoon clear honey

4 slices thick cut hickory smoked bacon

2 tablespoons extra virgin olive oil

4 large eggs

salt and cracked black pepper

tomato ketchup and hash browns (page 29), to serve (optional)

serves 4

Mix the mustard and honey together and brush over the bacon slices. Broil for 2–3 minutes on each side, until cooked through. Cover loosely with aluminum foil and keep them warm while cooking the eggs.

Heat the oil in a skillet until really hot. Add the eggs, 2 at a time, and cook until the whites are bubbly and crisp-looking. Put an egg on top of each bacon slice. Sprinkle with salt and pepper and serve with tomato ketchup and some hash browns, if using.

creamy
scrambled eggs
with goat cheese

Stirring a little creamy goat cheese into lightly scrambled eggs transforms a simple dish into a delicious light lunch. The nasturtium flowers are optional, but they do add a delightful flash of color as well as a delicate, peppery flavor.

serves 4

12 eggs

½ cup light cream

2 tablespoons chopped fresh marjoram or thyme

4 tablespoons butter

6 oz. goat cheese, diced

a handful of nasturtium flowers, torn (optional)

salt and cracked black pepper

toasted walnut bread, to serve

Put the eggs in a bowl and beat in the cream, marjoram or thyme, and a little salt and pepper. Melt the butter in a nonstick saucepan, add the eggs, and stir over a low heat until the eggs are just beginning to set.

Stir in the goat cheese and continue to cook briefly, still stirring, until the cheese melts into the eggs. Add the nasturtium flowers, if using, and spoon onto the toast. Serve immediately.

charred asparagus and herb frittata

with smoked salmon

Charring the asparagus spears on a stove-top grill pan intensifies their flavor and adds a smokiness to the frittata.

8 oz. asparagus spears

1 tablespoon extra virgin olive oil

6 eggs

4 scallions, finely chopped

2 tablespoons chopped fresh herbs, such as tarragon, dill, and mint

¼ cup fresh ricotta

1 tablespoon butter

8 oz. smoked salmon

salt and cracked black pepper

to serve

sour cream or crème fraîche

lemon wedges

serves 4

Trim the asparagus and toss with the oil and a little salt and pepper. Heat a stove-top grill pan until hot, add the asparagus, and cook for 3–4 minutes, turning until evenly charred. Set aside to cool.

Put the eggs in a bowl and beat until evenly mixed. Stir in the scallions, herbs, and ricotta. Add salt and pepper to taste.

Melt the butter in a large nonstick skillet, add the egg mixture, and swirl to the edge of the pan. Arrange the asparagus spears over the top and cook for 3–4 minutes until set underneath.

Put briefly under a hot broiler to cook the surface, then let cool to room temperature.

Cut into slices and serve with the smoked salmon, sour cream or crème fraîche, and lemon wedges.

salmon and sweet potato fishcakes

I love fishcakes, and these, made with sweet potatoes, are a particular favorite.

1 lb. salmon fillets

1 tablespoon olive oil

1 lb. sweet potatoes, peeled and cubed

4 scallions, finely chopped

1 small garlic clove, crushed

grated zest and juice of ½ lemon

⅓ cup fine cornmeal

sunflower oil, for frying

salt and freshly ground black pepper

green salad, to serve

lemon and rosemary mayonnaise

leaves from 1 sprig of rosemary

½ teaspoon salt

2 egg yolks

1 teaspoon Dijon mustard

1¼ cups olive oil

1–2 tablespoons freshly squeezed lemon juice

serves 4

Put the salmon fillets on a sheet of aluminum foil and drizzle with the oil. Wrap the foil loosely around the salmon and bake in a preheated oven at 400°F for 20–25 minutes. Remove from the oven and leave until cold. Flake the flesh with a fork, reserving any juices from the package.

Cook the potatoes in lightly salted, boiling water for 15 minutes. Drain well, return to the saucepan, and dry out briefly over a low heat. Mash coarsely with a fork and set aside to cool.

Add the fish with the juices, scallions, garlic, lemon zest, and juice to the cooled potatoes. Add salt and pepper to taste and mix well. Shape into 8 small cakes and refrigerate for 30 minutes.

To make the mayonnaise, pound the rosemary leaves and salt to a coarse powder with a mortar and pestle. Put in a food processor with the egg yolks and mustard and blend briefly. With the motor running, gradually add the oil through the funnel until thickened and glossy. Add lemon juice to taste.

Coat the fishcakes with cornmeal. Put enough oil to cover the base of a skillet and heat until hot. Add the fishcakes and sauté for 4–5 minutes on each side until golden. Serve with the mayonnaise and a green salad.

A simple fruit compote that I prefer to serve slightly warm. Add whatever extra berries you fancy.

warm compote

with peaches, apricots, and blueberries

2 oranges

2 lb. any combination of ripe peaches, nectarines, and fresh apricots

⅔ cup blueberries

2 tablespoons sugar

1 cinnamon stick

yogurt, to serve

serves 4

Peel the zest from 1 of the oranges, being careful not to get any of the bitter white pith. Cut the zest into thin strips, and put in a shallow saucepan. Squeeze the juice from both oranges and add to the saucepan.

Cut the peaches or nectarines into slices and the apricots in half. Add to the pan with the sugar and cinnamon stick and heat gently until the sugar dissolves. Cover and simmer gently for 4–5 minutes, until the fruits are softened.

Remove from the heat. Serve warm with yogurt.

sweet things

baby custard tarts

with cardamom coffee

This recipe is inspired by the little custard tarts ("pasteis de nata") found all over Portugal.

Using the cookie cutter or a glass, stamp out 24 rounds from the rolled out pastry or pie crust. Press the rounds carefully into the muffin pans, lightly prick the pastry bases, and line each base with a circle of wax paper.

Fill the pastry bases with baking beans (or rice if you don't have baking beans) and bake in an oven preheated to 400°F for 5 minutes. Remove the paper and beans and return to the oven for a few more minutes to crisp. Set aside and reduce the oven temperature to 300°F.

Meanwhile, to make the filling, put the milk, sugar, and vanilla extract in a saucepan and bring to a boil. Simmer until reduced by about half. Put the egg yolks, whole egg, and cornstarch in a bowl and beat well. Gradually beat in the vanilla milk. Pour the mixture into the tart shells and bake for 10 minutes, until the surface of the custard is glossy and the centers are just set. Set aside until cold.

To make the coffee, remove the seeds from the cardamom pods and grind with the coffee beans, in a coffee grinder. Use the ground cardamom coffee to make espresso in the normal way. Dust the tarts with cinnamon and serve with a small cup of the spiced coffee.

Note: to make 10 oz. pastry dough, put 1 cup all-purpose flour, a pinch of salt, ¾ stick butter and 2 tablespoons sugar in a food processor and process to fine crumbs. With the machine running add 1 egg yolk and 1-2 tablespoons ice water until the dough comes together. Wrap and chill for 30 minutes before rolling out on a lightly floured surface.

10 oz. sweet pastry dough (see below) or refrigerated pie crust, rolled out enough to yield 24 rounds of dough

1¼ cups milk

⅓ cup sugar

1 teaspoon vanilla extract

2 egg yolks

1 whole egg

½ tablespoon cornstarch

ground cinnamon, to dust

cardamom coffee

3 cardamom pods

4 tablespoons espresso coffee beans

3-inch cookie cutter

two 12-cup muffin tins or jam tart trays

baking beans or rice

makes 24

pecan and chocolate muffins

I use good quality dark chocolate, chopped up, rather than chocolate chips, as it has a much better flavor and texture.

1½ cups self-rising flour

1 teaspoon baking powder

2½ oz. pecans, finely ground

⅔ cup brown sugar

1 egg

¼ cup maple syrup

1 cup milk

4 tablespoons butter, melted

3¼ oz. dark chocolate, coarsely chopped into very small pieces

chopped pecans, to decorate

one 12-cup muffin tin, lined with paper cases

makes 12

Sift the flour and baking powder into a bowl and stir in the pecans and sugar. Put the egg, maple syrup, milk, and melted butter into a second bowl and beat well. Beat into the dry ingredients, then fold in the chocolate pieces.

Spoon the mixture into the paper cases, sprinkling the surface with extra chopped pecans.

Bake in a preheated oven at 400°F for 18–20 minutes, until risen and golden. Cool on a wire rack and serve warm.

walnut cake
with coffee syrup

Coffee and walnuts are wonderful together, and this is a perfect way to combine them. Drizzling the nutty sponge with a spiced coffee syrup leaves it deliciously moist and gooey.

6 eggs, separated

¾ cup sugar

2½ cups walnut halves, finely ground in a food processor

¾ cup day-old bread crumbs

whipped cream, to serve

coffee syrup

1¼ cups strong black coffee

½ cup sugar

3 star anise

9-inch springform pan, greased and lined with a round of greased parchment

serves 8

Put the egg yolks into a large bowl, add ⅔ cup of the sugar and whisk until pale. Stir in the ground walnuts and bread crumbs. (The mixture will be very stiff at this stage.)

Whisk the egg whites in a separate bowl until soft peaks form, then gradually whisk in the remaining sugar. Stir a large spoonful into the cake mixture, then fold in the rest until evenly mixed. Spoon into the prepared cake pan and bake in an oven preheated to 350°F for 35–40 minutes, until risen and springy to the touch.

Meanwhile, put the coffee, sugar, and star anise in a saucepan. Heat until the sugar dissolves, then boil for 5–6 minutes until syrupy. Cool slightly.

Using a wooden toothpick, spike the cake all over the surface and drizzle with half the syrup. Set aside to cool slightly. Serve the cake still warm with lightly whipped cream and the remaining coffee syrup spooned around it in a pool.

sweet
bruschetta
with quince-glazed figs

Quince paste is available from gourmet stores, or alternatively use raspberry preserve or red currant jelly.

2 tablespoons quince paste

2 tablespoons butter

2 tablespoons port

12 ripe figs, halved

4 slices of brioche loaf or challah

confectioners' sugar and cinnamon, to dust

yogurt, to serve

serves 4

Put the quince paste, butter, and port in a saucepan and heat gently until melted. Arrange the figs, cut side up, in an ovenproof dish. Spoon over the port mixture, making sure the surface of each fig is well covered.

Put under a hot broiler and cook for 3–5 minutes, until the figs are caramelized and heated through.

Meanwhile, toast the brioche or challah on a stove-top grill pan. Transfer to heated serving plates and sprinkle immediately with confectioner's sugar and cinnamon.

Top with the figs and serve with yogurt.

iced bloody mary

Wonderful, with or without a hangover!

1¼ cups iced Stolichnaya or Absolut vodka

2½ cups tomato juice

juice of 1 lemon

¼ cup Worcestershire sauce

½–1 teaspoon Tabasco sauce

2½ cups crushed ice

serves 2–3

Put all the ingredients in a blender and pulse briefly to a coarse purée. Transfer to a bowl and freeze for about 1–1½ hours, until slushy and slightly icy. Using an electric or a balloon whisk, beat briefly to soften. The mixture should be creamy but just liquid enough to pass through a straw. Transfer to glasses and serve with short straws.

drinks

iced coffee

This iced coffee can also be served black.

2½ cups freshly made espresso coffee

sugar (optional)

milk

serves 2

Chill the freshly made espresso coffee, sweetened with sugar, if using. Pour into chilled glasses, adding a few ice cubes. Top up with a little milk and serve.

mocha affogato

"Affogato" is Italian for "drowned," here referring to the ice cream which is drowned in coffee. Use good quality ice cream.

4 small scoops chocolate ice cream

4 small scoops vanilla ice cream

freshly made espresso coffee

serves 4

Divide the ice cream between 4 chilled coffee cups, top up with the hot coffee and serve.

ginger and lemon tisane

This lightly spiced tisane has a wonderful cleansing effect on the body—an ideal start to the day.

2 inches fresh ginger, peeled

2 stalks lemongrass

4 teaspoons honey

1 lemon, sliced

serves 4

Thinly slice the ginger and cut each lemongrass stalk in half crosswise, then lengthwise. Put the ginger and lemongrass into cups, then add the honey and a slice of lemon. Top up with boiling water and serve.

champagne cocktails

There is something decidedly decadent about a glass of fizz in the morning, so if you're going to treat yourself to brunch, why not totally spoil yourself with one of these cocktails.

campari fizz

6 shots of Campari

3 teaspoons sugar

1 bottle chilled sparkling wine, 750 ml

serves 6

Pour the Campari into champagne flutes and sweeten each with ½ teaspoon sugar. Top up with sparkling wine and serve.

peach bellini

3 ripe peaches

1 bottle chilled Prosecco or sparkling wine, 750 ml

serves 6

Peel the peaches by plunging them into boiling water for 30 seconds. Refresh them under cold water and peel off the skin. Cut in half, remove the pit, and chop the flesh.

Put the peaches into a blender, add a small amount of Prosecco, and process to a purée. Pour into glasses and top up with the remaining Prosecco.

mimosa

6 blood oranges or ordinary oranges

1 bottle chilled sparkling wine, 750 ml

serves 6

Squeeze the oranges and divide the juice between 6 glasses. Top up with wine and serve.

cool drinks

Fruit and yogurt drinks are packed full of goodness and vitality and could almost be served as a meal in themselves. When really ripe mangoes are unavailable, canned mango purée, available from Asian stores, makes a great alternative.

raspberry and rosewater yogurt drink

1½ cups raspberries

¼ cup rosewater

1¼ cups plain yogurt

2–3 tablespoons honey

12 ice cubes

serves 4

Put all the ingredients in a blender. Blend to a purée and serve.

mango, coconut, and passion fruit shake

1 large mango, peeled, or 1¼ cups mango purée

6 large passion fruit, or ⅔ cup passion fruit juice

¾ cup coconut milk

12 ice cubes

serves 4

Cut the mango flesh away from the pit. Coarsely chop the flesh and put into a blender. Cut the passion fruit in half and scoop the seeds into a strainer set over a bowl. Use a spoon to press down the seeds and extract all the juice. Add the juice, coconut milk, and ice cubes to the blender and purée until smooth.

conversion charts

Weights and measures have been rounded up or down slightly to make measuring easier.

Volume equivalents:

American	Metric	Imperial
1 teaspoon	5 ml	
1 tablespoon	15 ml	
¼ cup	60 ml	2 fl.oz.
⅓ cup	75 ml	2½ fl.oz.
½ cup	125 ml	4 fl.oz.
⅔ cup	150 ml	5 fl.oz. (¼ pint)
¾ cup	175 ml	6 fl.oz.
1 cup	250 ml	8 fl.oz.

Weight equivalents:

Imperial	Metric
1 oz.	25 g
2 oz.	50 g
3 oz.	75 g
4 oz.	125 g
5 oz.	150 g
6 oz.	175 g
7 oz.	200 g
8 oz. (½ lb.)	250 g
9 oz.	275 g
10 oz.	300 g
11 oz.	325 g
12 oz.	375 g
13 oz.	400 g
14 oz.	425 g
15 oz.	475 g
16 oz. (1 lb.)	500 g
2 lb.	1 kg

Measurements:

Inches	Cm
¼ inch	5 mm
½ inch	1 cm
¾ inch	1.5 cm
1 inch	2.5 cm
2 inches	5 cm
3 inches	7 cm
4 inches	10 cm
5 inches	12 cm
6 inches	15 cm
7 inches	18 cm
8 inches	20 cm
9 inches	23 cm
10 inches	25 cm
11 inches	28 cm
12 inches	30 cm

Oven temperatures:

110°C	(225°F)	Gas ¼
120°C	(250°F)	Gas ½
140°C	(275°F)	Gas 1
150°C	(300°F)	Gas 2
160°C	(325°F)	Gas 3
180°C	(350°F)	Gas 4
190°C	(375°F)	Gas 5
200°C	(400°F)	Gas 6
220°C	(425°F)	Gas 7
230°C	(450°F)	Gas 8
240°C	(475°F)	Gas 9

index